table of contents

·······································

Salads

Pastas

Recipes used with permission. © Meredith Corporation. All Rights Reserved.
Published in 2013 by Dalmatian Press, LLC. Printed in China.
The DALMATIAN PRESS name is a trademark of Dalmatian Publishing Group, Franklin, Tennessee 37067. 1-866-418-2572.
No part of this book may be reproduced or copied in any form without the written permission from the copyright owner.
All rights reserved.   CE16797 College Bites! Feeding U: Salads and Pastas

greek salad

TOTAL TIME: 15 MINUTES | SERVINGS: 6

For a quick vibrant salad, make the Greek vinaigrette ahead of time and store it in the fridge so it will be ready to toss with greens, olives, and feta cheese.

You will need

- ☐ 6 cups torn mixed salad greens or romaine
- ☐ 2 medium tomatoes, cut into wedges, or 8 cherry tomatoes, halved
- ☐ 1 cucumber, halved lengthwise and thinly sliced *No*
- ☐ 1 red onion, cut into thin wedges
- ☐ ½ cup pitted kalamata olives
- ☐ ½ cup crumbled feta cheese
- ☐ Greek vinaigrette

1. In a salad bowl, combine salad greens, tomatoes, cucumber, onion, olives, and crumbled cheese. Add Greek vinaigrette; toss to coat.

2. **Greek vinaigrette**: In a screw top jar, combine 2 tablespoons olive oil or salad oil; 2 tablespoons lemon juice; 2 teaspoons snipped fresh oregano or ½ teaspoon dried oregano, crushed; $\frac{1}{8}$ teaspoon salt; and $\frac{1}{8}$ teaspoon black pepper. Cover and shake well.

jumping black bean salad

TOTAL TIME: 15 MINUTES **| SERVINGS:** 3

In this main-dish salad, red pepper and cumin add spice, while black beans bring protein to the mix. Serve it with crusty bread for a cool meal on a hot day.

You will need

- 1 (15-ounce) can black beans, rinsed and drained
- 2 teaspoons olive oil
- ½ teaspoon ground cumin
- 2 tablespoons lime juice
- 4 cups torn mixed greens
- 1 tomato, chopped
- ½ cup shredded carrots
- salt
- ground red pepper

Stir together black beans, olive oil, cumin, and lime juice; set aside. In a large bowl, toss together greens, tomato, and carrot; add bean mixture and toss to mix. Season to taste with salt and red pepper.

mixed greens and fruit salad

· ·

TOTAL TIME: 15 MINUTES | **SERVINGS:** 4

Enjoy this tossed green salad with fresh berries in the summer months or with canned mandarin orange sections during the winter.

You will need

- ☐ 4 cups torn mixed greens
- ☐ 1 cup sliced fresh mushrooms
- ☐ 1 cup fresh blueberries, raspberries, quartered strawberries, and/or canned mandarin orange sections, drained

- ☐ ⅓ cup orange juice
- ☐ 4 teaspoons salad oil
- ☐ 4 teaspoons brown mustard
- ☐ 1 ½ teaspoons sugar
- ☐ 1 ½ snipped fresh mint or ¼ teaspoon dried mint, crushed

- ☐ ¼ teaspoon salt
- ☐ ⅛ teaspoon ground black pepper

1. In a large bowl, gently toss together the salad greens, mushrooms, and fruit.

2. For dressing, in a screw-top jar combine orange juice, oil, brown mustard, sugar, mint, salt, and pepper. Cover and shake until combined. Drizzle over salad. Toss gently to coat.

pineapple coleslaw

TOTAL TIME: 10 MINUTES | SERVINGS: 4

Try this sweet coleslaw as a side dish when you want a change from the traditional savory version.

You will need

- ☐ 1 ½ cups packaged shredded cabbage with carrots (coleslaw mix)
- ☐ ¼ cup well-drained pineapple tidbits
- ☐ 2 tablespoons vanilla low-fat yogurt
- ☐ 2 tablespoons light mayonnaise dressing or salad dressing
- ☐ ¼ cup honey-roasted peanuts, chopped

In a small bowl, combine cabbage, pineapple, yogurt, and mayonnaise dressing; toss to mix. Sprinkle with peanuts.

trattoria-style spinach fettuccine

TOTAL TIME: 20 MINUTES | SERVINGS: 4

This fettuccine recipe is the type of soulful pasta dish that neighborhood trattorias take pride in serving. It tosses intensely flavored double-tomato sauce with tangy feta cheese for a dinner that demands a red-checked tablecloth and candles.

You will need

- 1 (9-ounce) package refrigerated spinach fettuccine
- 2 tablespoons chopped shallot or green onion
- 1 medium carrot, coarsely shredded (about ½ cup)
- ¼ cup oil-packed dried tomatoes, drained and snipped
- 1 tablespoon olive oil
- 4 medium red and/or yellow tomatoes, coarsely chopped (2 ⅔ cups)
- ½ cup crumbled garlic and herb or peppercorn feta cheese

1. Using kitchen scissors, cut the stack of fettuccine strands in half crosswise (for easier eating). Cook the pasta according to package directions; drain. Return pasta to hot pan.

2. Meanwhile, in a large skillet, cook shallot and carrots in hot oil over medium heat for 1 to 2 minutes, or until just tender. Stir in fresh and dried tomatoes; cook 1 to 2 minutes or until heated through. Spoon tomato mixture over cooked pasta; toss gently. Sprinkle with cheese.

bow ties with sausage and peppers

TOTAL TIME: 25 MINUTES | **SERVINGS:** 4

It's hard to believe this delicious sausage, sweet pepper, and pasta main dish recipe takes under 30 minutes to prepare.

You will need

- ☐ 1 (8-ounce) package dried large bow ties
- ☐ 12 ounces spicy Italian sausage links
- ☐ 2 medium red sweet peppers, cut into ¾-inch pieces
- ☐ ½ cup vegetable broth or beef broth
- ☐ ¼ teaspoon coarsely ground black pepper
- ☐ ¼ cup snipped flat-leaf parsley

1. Cook pasta according to package directions. Drain; keep warm.

2. Meanwhile, cut the sausage into 1-inch pieces. In a large skillet, cook sausage and sweet peppers over medium-high heat until sausage is brown. Drain.

3. Add the broth and black pepper to skillet. Bring to boiling; reduce heat. Simmer, uncovered, for 5 minutes. Remove from heat. Pour over pasta; add parsley. Stir gently to coat.

ravioli skillet

This one-pan wonder is fast, nutritious, and delicious.

You will need

- ☐ 1 (14.5-ounce) can Italian-style stewed tomatoes, undrained
- ☐ 1 (14-ounce) can vegetable broth
- ☐ 2 zucchini, halved lengthwise and sliced ½ inch thick (about 2½ cups)
- ☐ 1 (9-ounce) package refrigerated cheese ravioli
- ☐ 1 (15-ounce) can white kidney beans (cannellini) or navy beans, rinsed and drained
- ☐ 2 tablespoons grated Parmesan cheese
- ☐ 2 tablespoons snipped fresh basil

1. In a large saucepan, combine tomatoes and broth; bring to boiling. Stir in zucchini and ravioli. Return to boiling; reduce heat. Boil gently, uncovered, for 6 to 7 minutes or until ravioli is tender and broth mixture is slightly thickened, stirring gently once or twice.

2. Stir beans into ravioli mixture; heat through. Sprinkle each serving with Parmesan cheese and basil.

chili macaroni

TOTAL TIME: 30 MINUTES | **SERVINGS:** 4

Wagon wheel macaroni and green beans replace the kidney beans in this ground beef and pasta dinner.

You will need

- ☐ 12 ounces lean ground beef or uncooked ground turkey
- ☐ ½ cup chopped onion
- ☐ 1 (14.5-ounce) can diced tomatoes and green chilies
- ☐ 1 ¼ cups tomato juice
- ☐ 2 teaspoons chili powder
- ☐ ½ teaspoon garlic salt
- ☐ 1 cup dried wagon wheel macaroni or elbow macaroni
- ☐ 1 cup frozen cut green beans
- ☐ 1 cup shredded Cheddar cheese
- ☐ Tortilla chips

1. In a very large skillet, cook ground beef and onion over medium heat until meat is brown. Drain off fat. Stir undrained tomatoes, tomato juice, chili powder, and garlic salt into meat mixture. Bring to boiling. Stir in pasta and green beans. Return to boiling; reduce heat. Cover and simmer about 15 minutes or until pasta and beans are tender.

2. Top with shredded Cheddar cheese and serve with tortilla chips, if desired.

spinach tortellini with beans and feta

TOTAL TIME: 18 MINUTES | **SERVINGS:** 4

This easy pasta main dish recipe will add a little pizzaz to your pasta. The mix of spinach, beans, veggies, and cheese is ready in less than 20 minutes.

You will need

- ☐ 1 (9-ounce) package refrigerated cheese-filled spinach tortellini
- ☐ 1 (15-ounce) can cannellini (white kidney) beans, rinsed and drained
- ☐ ¾ cup crumbled garlic-and-herb-flavored feta cheese
- ☐ 2 tablespoons olive oil
- ☐ 1 large tomato, chopped
- ☐ ground black pepper
- ☐ 4 cups baby spinach

1. Cook tortellini according to package directions. Drain and return to pan.

2. Add drained beans, feta cheese, and olive oil to tortellini in saucepan. Cook over medium heat until beans are hot and cheese begins to melt, gently stirring occasionally. Add tomato; cook 1 minute more. Sprinkle with black pepper.

3. Place 1 cup of baby spinach on plate or shallow bowl. Top with tortellini mixture

fast chicken fettuccine

TOTAL TIME: 20 MINUTES | SERVINGS: 4

This fast fettuccine packs in the protein for a hearty meal.

You will need

- ☐ 8 ounces fettuccine
- ☐ ¼ of a 7-ounce jar oil-packed, dried tomato strips or pieces (¼ cup)
- ☐ black pepper, freshy ground
- ☐ ½ pound skinless, boneless chicken breast, cut into strips
- ☐ ½ cup finely shredded Parmesan, Romano, or Asiago cheese
- ☐ 1 zucchini or yellow summer squash, halved lengthwise and sliced

1. Cook pasta in lightly salted boiling water according to package directions; drain. Return pasta to hot pan.

2. Meanwhile, drain tomato strips, reserving 2 tablespoons oil from jar; set aside. In a large skillet, heat 1 tablespoon reserved oil over medium-high heat. Add zucchini; cook and stir 2 to 3 minutes or until crisp-tender. Remove from skillet. Add remaining reserved oil to skillet. Add chicken; cook and stir 2 to 3 minutes or until no longer pink. Add zucchini, chicken, tomato strips, and cheese to cooked pasta; toss gently to combine. Season with pepper to taste.

pasta primavera with asparagus

TOTAL TIME: 17 MINUTES | SERVINGS: 4

This quick meatless pasta meal is flavored with a simple tomato sauce.

You will need

- ☐ 16 thin stalks fresh asparagus
- ☐ 8 ounces dried long fusili or ziti pasta
- ☐ 1 tablespoon olive oil
- ☐ ¼ cup shredded fresh basil
- ☐ 2 teaspoons bottled minced garlic
- ☐ ¼ teaspoon freshly ground white pepper
- ☐ ¼ teaspoon salt
- ☐ ¼ cup water
- ☐ 1 tablespoon butter or margarine
- ☐ 3 small red, orange, and/or yellow tomatoes, seeded and cut up

1. Snap off and discard woody bases of fresh asparagus. Rinse. Cut or snap off the tips; set aside. Bias-slice asparagus stalks into 1- to 1 ½-inch pieces; set aside.

2. Cook pasta according to package directions. Meanwhile, heat oil in a large skillet over medium heat. Add garlic and pepper; cook and stir for 30 seconds.Remove from skillet.

3. Add asparagus stalk pieces, water, and salt to skillet. Bring to boiling; reduce heat. Cook, uncovered, for 3 minutes or until asparagus is crisp-tender, stirring occasionally. Add tomatoes and asparagus tips; cook, uncovered, for 1 minute more or until the tomatoes are heated through. Remove from heat; stir in butter.

4. Drain pasta; add pasta and basil to vegetables in skillet. Toss gently to combine.

pasta with tomato

TOTAL TIME: 20 MINUTES | **SERVINGS:** 4

This fresh pasta sauce recipe is the essence of simplicity. Chopped Roma tomatoes, lightly sauteed in olive oil and seasoned with basil, are tossed with hot cooked rotini and topped with grated cheese.

You will need

- ☐ 4 ounces dried rotini or fusilli
- ☐ 2 cups coarsely chopped plum tomatoes
- ☐ 2 tablespoons olive oil
- ☐ ¼ teaspoon salt
- ☐ 3 tablespoons shredded fresh basil
- ☐ ¼ cup shaved or grated Parmesan or Romano cheese
- ☐ ¼ teaspoon pepper

1. Cook the pasta according to package directions; drain.

2. Meanwhile, in a saucepan, combine tomatoes, olive oil, and salt. Cook over medium-low heat until heated through and tomatoes start to juice-out slightly. Stir in the basil.

3. Divide pasta among 4 plates. Top each serving with some of the tomato mixture. Sprinkle with cheese and pepper.

quick skillet lasagna

TOTAL TIME: 30 MINUTES | **SERVINGS:** 6

Talk about quick! Just cook the pasta, then prepare this lasagna in a skillet.

You will need

- ☐ 3 cups (6 ounces) dried mafalda (mini lasagna) noodles
- ☐ 12 ounces lean ground beef
- ☐ 1 (26- to 27 ¾ ounce) jar tomato-base pasta sauce
- ☐ 1 ½ cups shredded mozzarella cheese
- ☐ ¼ cup grated Parmesan cheese

1. Cook pasta according to package directions; drain.

2. Meanwhile, cook meat in a 10-inch nonstick skillet until meat is brown; drain. Set meat aside. Wipe skillet with paper towel.

3. Spread about half of the cooked pasta in the skillet. Cover with about half of the sauce. Spoon cooked meat over sauce. Sprinkle with 1 cup of the mozzarella cheese. Top with remaining pasta and sauce. Sprinkle remaining mozzarella and Parmesan cheese over top.

4. Cook, covered, over medium heat for 5 to 7 minutes or until heated through and cheese melts. Remove skillet from heat and let stand, covered, for 1 minute.

ham and peas macaroni 'n' cheese

TOTAL TIME: 25 MINUTES | **SERVINGS:** 8

This creamy mac 'n' cheese main dish is brimming with chunks of deli ham and wagon wheel pasta.

You will need

- [ ] 8 ounces large wagon wheel pasta or elbow macaroni
- [ ] 2 cups frozen peas
- [ ] ¾ cup milk
- [ ] 2 (6 ½-ounce) containers light semi-soft cheese with garlic and herb
- [ ] 12 ounces cooked ham or cooked chicken, cut into chunks
- [ ] ½ cup shredded Cheddar cheese

In a large pot, cook pasta according to package directions. Stir in peas last minute. Drain pasta mixture; return to pot. Add milk, soft cheese, ham, and Cheddar cheese. Cook and stir until heated through.

tortellini soup

Cream cheese and tomato soup make a rich and creamy base for this four-ingredient tortellini soup recipe that can be prepared in just 15 minutes.

You will need

- ☐ 2 (14-ounce) cans reduced-sodium chicken broth or vegetable broth
- ☐ 1 (9-ounce) package refrigerated tortellini
- ☐ ½ of an 8-ounce tub cream cheese spread with chive and onion
- ☐ 1 (10.75- or 11- ounce) can condensed tomato bisque soup

In a medium saucepan, bring broth to boiling. Add tortellini; reduce heat. Simmer, uncovered, for 5 minutes. In a bowl, whisk ⅓ cup of the hot broth into the cream cheese spread until smooth. Return all to saucepan along with tomato soup; heat through.

penne with meat sauce

TOTAL TIME: 25 MINUTES | SERVINGS: 6

Quick-to-grab ingredients make this hearty ground beef and pasta dish super easy.

You will need

- ☐ 8 ounces dried penne
- ☐ 1 pound lean ground beef
- ☐ ½ cup chopped onion
- ☐ 1 (14-ounce) can whole Italian-style tomatoes, undrained

- ☐ ½ of a 6-ounce can Italian-style tomato paste
- ☐ ¼ cup tomato juice
- ☐ ½ teaspoon sugar
- ☐ ½ teaspoon dried oregano, crushed

- ☐ ¼ teaspoon ground black pepper
- ☐ ¼ cup sliced pitted ripe olives
- ☐ ½ cup shredded reduced-fat mozzarella cheese

1. Cook pasta according to package directions. Drain well. Return pasta to hot pan; cover to keep warm.

2. Meanwhile, in a very large skillet, cook ground beef and onion until meat is brown. Drain off fat. In a blender, combine undrained tomatoes, tomato paste, sugar, dried oregano, and pepper. Cover and blend until smooth.

3. Stir tomato mixture into meat mixture in skillet. Bring to boiling; reduce heat. Cover and simmer for 10 minutes. Stir in cooked pasta and olives. Cover and heat through.

4. Sprinkle with mozzarella cheese.

linguine with garlic

TOTAL TIME: 30 MINUTES | SERVINGS: 8

Serve this flavorful pasta dish with a healthy green vegetable.

You will need

have to try

- ☐ 2 slices white bread
- ☐ 8 ounces linguine
- ☐ 3 tablespoons butter or margarine
- ☐ 2 tablespoons olive oil
- ☐ 3 cloves garlic, finely chopped
- ☐ ¼ cup grated Romano or Parmesan cheese
- ☐ pepper
- ☐ 2 tablespoons snipped parsley

1. Place bread in a blender container bowl. Blend until coarse crumbs are produced. Measure ¾ cup and set aside.

2. Cook pasta according to package directions; drain. Toss pasta with butter or margarine. Cover and keep warm.

3. Heat the olive oil in a large skillet over medium heat. Add the garlic and stir constantly for 30 seconds. Add the bread crumbs and cook, turning often with a spatula, until the crumbs are golden brown (about 5 minutes). Watch carefully to avoid burning the mixture.

4. Add the pasta. Turn gently to coat with the crumb mixture; heat through. Remove the skillet from the heat and add the Romano or Parmesan cheese. Add pepper to taste. Toss gently to combine. Sprinkle with parsley.

chicken and bow ties

TOTAL TIME: 30 MINUTES | SERVINGS: 4

A rich cheese sauce tops chicken and pasta in this simple, yet elegant, dinner.

You will need

- ☐ 8 ounces dried bow tie pasta
- ☐ 2 cloves garlic, minced
- ☐ 2 tablespoons olive oil
- ☐ 1 pound skinless, boneless chicken breast halves, cut into thin bite-size strips

- ☐ 1 teaspoon dried basil, crushed
- ☐ ⅛ teaspoon crushed red pepper
- ☐ ½ cup oil-packed dried tomatoes, drained and cut into thin strips

- ☐ ¾ cup chicken broth
- ☐ ¼ cup water
- ☐ ½ cup whipping cream
- ☐ ¼ cup grated Parmesan cheese

1. Cook pasta according to package directions; drain.

2. Meanwhile, in a large skillet, cook the garlic in hot oil over medium-high heat for 30 seconds. Add chicken, basil, and crushed red pepper. Cook and stir for 4 minutes or until browned. Add chicken broth, dried tomatoes, and water. Bring to boiling; reduce heat. Simmer, uncovered, about 10 minutes or until chicken is tender and no longer pink. Stir in whipping cream and the ¼ cup Parmesan cheese; simmer for 2 minutes more. Stir pasta into chicken mixture. Heat through.

smoky mushroom stroganoff

TOTAL TIME: 18 MINUTES | **SERVINGS:** 4

A creamy mushroom sauce tops egg noodles in this vegetarian twist on a classic Italian favorite.

You will need

- ☐ 1 (8.8-ounce) package dried pappardelle (wide egg noodles)
- ☐ 1 ½ pound package sliced mushrooms, such as button, cremini, and/or shiitake
- ☐ 2 cloves garlic, minced
- ☐ 1 tablespoon olive oil
- ☐ 1 (8-ounce) carton light sour cream
- ☐ 2 tablespoons all-purpose flour
- ☐ 1 ½ teaspoons smoked paprika
- ☐ 1 cup vegetable broth

1. Cook noodles according to package directions. Drain; keep warm.

2. In extra-large skillet, cook mushrooms and garlic in hot oil over medium-high heat 5-8 minutes or until tender, stirring occasionally. (Reduce heat if mushrooms brown quickly.) Remove with slotted spoon; cover to keep warm.

3. For sauce, in bowl combine sour cream, flour, paprika, and ¼ teaspoon pepper. Stir in broth until smooth. Add to skillet. Cook and stir until thick and bubbly; cook and stir 1 minute more. Serve mushroom mixture and sauce over noodles.